The Foreign Policy Ce

www.fpc.org.uk

The Foreign Policy Centre is an independent think-tank committed to developing innovative thinking and effective solutions for our increasingly interdependent world. We aim to broaden perceptions of what foreign policy is, revitalise public debate about foreign policy goals and find new ways to get people involved. The Foreign Policy Centre publishes books and reports, organises high-profile conferences, public lectures and seminars, and runs major in-house research programmes on cross-cutting international issues.

For details of current and forthcoming publications, please see the back of this pamphlet. Individual publications should be ordered from:
Central Books, 99 Wallis Road, London E9 5LN
T + 44 (0)20 8986 5488 F + 44 (0)20 8533 5821

For further information about the Centre, including subscriptions, please visit our website or contact us at info@fpc.org.uk

voice of the voluntary sector

The National Council for Voluntary Organisations (NCVO) is the umbrella body for the voluntary sector in England. NCVO's vision is of a fair and open society which encourages and is supported by voluntary action. It aims to give a shared voice to voluntary organisations, to cultivate an environment that fosters their development, to help voluntary organisations to achieve the highest standards of practice and effectiveness and to provide leadership to the voluntary sector in tackling new issues and unmet needs.

NCVO has a growing membership of 1,500 voluntary organisations, ranging from large national bodies to community groups, volunteer bureaux and development agencies working at local level.

NGO Rights and Responsibilities
A New Deal for Global Governance

'A smart and insightful account of the changing role of NGOs in global politics, offering not only a significant analysis of NGO activity today, but a series of excellent policy recommendations to encourage innovation and improvement in NGO participation in global governance'.
David Held, *Professor of Politics, Open University*

'This is a timely and thought-provoking pamphlet. Mike Edwards writes from considerable and varied experience and this shows in the balance, objectivity, great good sense and flashes of humour which he brings to bear on this important, and too often polarised, debate'.
David Bryer, *Director, Oxfam*

About the author

Michael Edwards is Director of the Ford Foundation's Governance and Civil Society Unit in New York. He was previously Senior Civil Society Specialist at the World Bank and Head of Research for Save the Children and has written widely on international cooperation, development and NGO-state relations. His most recent book is *Future Positive: International Co-operation in the 21st Century*, published by Earthscan in the UK and Stylus in the US.

The views expressed in this report are those of the author alone and should not be taken as those of the Ford Foundation.

NGO Rights and Responsibilities

A New Deal for Global Governance

Michael Edwards

The Foreign Policy Centre

in association with

First published in 2000 by
The Foreign Policy Centre
Elizabeth House
(Mezzanine Floor)
39 York Road
London
SE1 7NQ
E info@fpc.org.uk
www.fpc.org.uk

Printed in Great Britain by
Bookcraft (Bath) Ltd

Cover and Design by
Interbrand Newell and Sorrell

NGO Rights and Responsibilities
A New Deal for Global Governance

1. Introduction:
Why we need a new deal in global governance

During the World Bank/IMF Annual meetings in Washington DC last autumn, I returned to my office to find two protestors sitting right outside my window. "Block the Chad-Cameroon pipeline", their banner read, in reference to a controversial loan under discussion at the time by the World Bank's Board of Directors. This was some achievement, since my office was on the fifth floor of the World Bank's headquarters – in true NGO spirit, the protestors had climbed up the steel cables that support the main entranceway and anchored themselves to the outside of my window frame (nothing personal, I hasten to add). Though more enterprising than the norm, such guests are increasingly frequent visitors to the World Bank and other international institutions. The growing profile of the NGO movement seems to herald a new era in world affairs when the voices of the poor will at last be heard around the global negotiating table. In recent years, NGOs have achieved some remarkable results, not just in pressurising the World Bank to reject the pipeline but in the Jubilee 2000 campaign against Third World debt, the worldwide ban on land mines agreed in Ottawa, and most recently, the disruption of trade talks during the 'battle of Seattle'. But these early efforts are just a taste of what lies ahead. Now is the time to give NGOs a formal role in global governance so that 'we the people' can play our proper part in shaping the century to come.

Or is it....?

Two days after my visitors had packed up their climbing gear, protestors were at it again, only this time they were demonstrating in favor of the pipeline, not against it. In contrast to the Washington-based lobbyists who made up the ranks of the critics, all of the pro-pipeline group were Africans – or at least gave a good impression of being so, dressed up in their traditional West African costumes and equipped with a veritable orchestra of drums: "Africans support World Bank participation in the Chad-Cameroon pipeline", their banner read, "as the only guarantee that the voices of the poor will be heard". The drummers were adding their voices to a growing chorus of complaint that sees NGOs as unrepresentative, unaccountable, and often plain uninformed – distorting the democratic process, eroding the authority of elected officials, and excluding the voices of those directly affected by global change in favor of an urban, middle-class minority of arm-chair radicals, based largely in the industrialised world. In the same week, Mats Karlsson, the World Bank's new Vice President for External Affairs, weighed in with a stinging attack on NGOs in Washington for their 'weak accountability', 'shallow democracy', and 'precarious legitimacy' as actors in the global debate. Having portrayed civil society in earlier times as something of a 'magic bullet' for all social, economic or political ills, attention is now turning to the failings (actual and perceived) of civil society itself. It is increasingly common to hear senior administrators, corporate executives, academics and journalists echo the complaints of many governments (especially in the developing world) that NGOs are self-selected, unaccountable and poorly rooted in society, thereby questioning their legitimacy as participants in global debates. The shape of governance is certainly changing, these critics say, but NGOs have no right to monopolise the popular voice. It's time they were put in their place.

Some observers celebrate the NGO phenomenon as heralding the birth of a true global democracy, while others worry about democracy's subversion by a growing web of special interests. So how should we respond to both the emerging power of NGOs and to the backlash that is gathering against them? Faced by the recent explosion of citizen protest around trade and globalization, it is tempting for politicians to close their eyes and hope that the demonstrators will go away: Brazilian Foreign Minister Luiz Felipe Lampreia has even suggested holding future meetings of the World Trade Organisation on a cruise ship, safely out of reach (offshore from Copacabana, perhaps?). But most people want a more positive solution, a way forward that recognises, structures and protects the role of ordinary citizens in influencing the decisions that affect their lives without undermining the essential authority of democratic government.

Neither the claims of the NGOs nor those of their critics can be taken at face value. The commitment and climbing ability of the anti-pipeline protestors outside my window does not in itself make their case any more or less valid. And, just as evidence later came to light that the African pro-pipeline protestors had been paid by corporations with a commercial interest in the project, we need to ask who is making the criticisms of NGOs and why. In part, NGOs are victims of their own success. Now that they have arrived as players on the world stage, the stakes are higher, and so is the temptation for their targets to fight back. "Business should challenge the NGO community to practice what they preach...if Washington and corporate America don't move decisively, NGOs could dominate public opinion on global trade and finance" wrote Jeffrey Garten, Dean of the Yale School of Management, in a recent issue of *Business Week*. But the backlash is no longer limited to voices from big business and the house journals of global finance. Many who would be thought of as natural friends and allies of the NGO movement – who saw its rise as providing more exciting and relevant ways to participate in response to dissatisfaction with traditional forms of politics – are also expressing increasing concerns. NGOs need to respond – not just because the gains they have made now seem under threat, but because broader hopes of reconstructing global governance could also be lost in a blame-game over the difficulties of international governance today.

This report seeks to break through the current impasse about the role of NGOs in global governance – to tackle and resolve these issues so that we can find a better way of answering the big questions facing tomorrow's global society. It outlines the background to these trends – looking at the reasons for the exponential growth in NGO activity and influence as the consensus on international development has shifted, as international organisations have sought to involve more actors to strengthen their own legitimacy, and as global governance has become more complex – and at the impact NGOs have been able to make as a result. It also examines why their growing influence is being challenged, and explores the dilemmas that lie ahead, unpacking what issues like 'representation' and 'accountability' should be taken to mean in the context of the growing power of the NGO movement.

And it proposes a New Deal between government and civil society actors in global governance. When 'global civil society' often seems little more than a marriage of convenience for disparate and often disaffected interests, there will be many practical difficulties. But we need to recognise that the emerging shape of global governance will not be neat or tidy; we are not heading towards a 'global government' but a complex patchwork quilt of agreements negotiated between governments, corporations and citizens' groups at different levels of the world system. While NGOs cannot and should not be expected to take the place of governments, they *will* have a voice in world affairs, and both they and their critics must find a way of harnessing that voice in more responsible and constructive ways as we seek to reshape global governance for the future. For governments and corporations, this may be the price of popular support for globalisation on a human scale.

I believe that this New Deal can be based on three main principles:

First, **the principle of *'a voice not a vote'*.** NGOs cannot claim to 'represent' the whole of civil society, but they can provide important avenues for a wider range of stakeholders to express their opinions. Their right to a voice should be promoted, structured to give every interest in civil society a fair and equal hearing, and developed from the bottom up so that global campaigns are built on strong local foundations. One way to do this would be through a set of 'compacts' between governments, businesses and NGO networks that lay out the roles and responsibilities of each set of actors around particular issues or institutions.

Second, participation in global governance should be granted in return for transparency and accountability on a set of **minimum standards for NGO integrity and performance,** monitored largely through self-regulation. Self-regulation has a long history in the NGO sector as an alternative to heavy-handed intervention by the state: the 'marshals' who added discipline to the civil rights movement in America and to anti-Vietnam war protests by students reappeared much later in Seattle, though in smaller numbers and with less success. Codes of conduct may be the best way to enforce a sense of self-discipline in global citizen action, perhaps with an international ombudsman or a quality assurance board to arbitrate in particularly difficult disputes.

Third, *a 'level playing field' for NGO involvement,* with special backing for voices that are currently left out of the global debate. That means additional support for capacity building, 'economic literacy', and financial autonomy among NGOs and other civil society groups in developing countries, and more opportunities to guarantee their direct participation in the international arena. This will mean sacrifices for the most powerful NGOs – but will strengthen their ability to put into practice their values and missions to empower others and make more space for their opinions.

Once we can get agreement on these broad principles, we will largely be able to leave civil societies to sort out the details by themselves. The conclusion to this report looks at what implementing these principles might mean in practice in key international organisations. These proposals will not solve all of the problems of NGO participation in global debates, but they can provide a basis for making global governance more effective and inclusive, and should help to assuage the criticisms that threaten to turn back the tide of global citizen action. The challenge for NGOs is to show that they can put into practice the principles that they campaign for in others, and genuinely add value to making international governance more effective. The challenge to governments is also clear: instead of opposing the rise of global civil society with tear gas, pepper spray and batons, put in place new rules of the game to ensure that its energies are channeled democratically, and to the genuine benefit of those who are excluded from the fruits of global progress.

2. The inexorable rise of NGOs

Before the fall of the Berlin Wall, 'civil society' raised little interest outside the cloisters of academic life. Today, the corridors of power reverberate with at least the rhetoric of partnership and citizen participation. And there is an increasingly heated political and media debate about the role of NGOs in which claims about their rights to representation are made and challenged. But, if this debate is to have a constructive outcome, we need it to be much clearer about what NGOs are, the reasons why their influence has increased, and the roles that they both can and should not be expected to play in the global governance system of the future. This chapter looks at why NGOs have risen so quickly up the international agenda – why has it been in the interests of governments, international organisations and NGOs to cooperate with each-other in the global arena? The next chapter examines the backlash against NGOs and how far it threatens to undo the gains that have been made to date.

What are NGOs?

One of the difficulties of generalising about NGOs is that 'NGOs' are so diverse. Sometimes they are conflated with 'civil society', the arena in which people come together to advance the interests they hold in common, not for profit or political power, but because they care enough about something to take collective action. But civil society includes all associations and networks between the family and the state except firms, so NGOs cannot 'represent' these interests as a whole. They are a sub-set of civic organisations, defined by the fact that they are formally registered with government, receive a significant proportion of their income from voluntary contributions (usually alongside grants from government), and are governed by a board of trustees rather than the elected representatives of a constituency. If civil society were an iceberg, then NGOs would be among the more noticeable of the peaks above the waterline, leaving the great bulk of community groups, informal associations, political parties and social networks sitting silently (but not passively) below. It is these groups and networks that are the true 'representatives' of civil society, not NGOs, and that is one reason why many NGOs are hurriedly strengthening their links with trade unions, consumer groups, peasant associations and the women's movement. But – by bridging and mediating between different levels and types of organisation – NGOs can help to provide the 'connective tissue' that holds different parts of civil society together.

Even so, NGOs come in all shapes and sizes, shades of political opinion, strategies, priorities and tactics, and some – like Amnesty International and Friends of the Earth – do have an active membership. NGOs in Europe and North America usually hit the headlines, but, in the aggregate, there are many more in the developing countries of the South than the North. Some NGOs are highly sophisticated lobbyists like Oxfam, while others (often church-based) concentrate on delivering services to those in need. Some are quiet and reformist – like CARE or the Christian NGO World Vision, while others are loud and deliberately confrontational, such as the World Development Movement and Global Exchange. Some NGOs believe that markets and trade – suitably re-shaped – are the best way to tackle global poverty, while others are fundamentally opposed to globalising capitalism in any shape or form. And although civil society is often seen as the key to future progressive politics, the civic arena contains many different interests and agendas, some of which are decidedly non-progressive. The US National Rifle Association has little in common with the peace marches of the Buddhist monk Ghosananda and his followers in Thailand, yet both are part of civil society in their respective countries – and the NRA has recently secured consultative status with the United Nations in New York. There is no such thing as a common set of civic interests that cross national borders, still less a global civil society with uniform goals and values.

These differences are very important in deciding how to deal with NGO involvement in global governance. The fact that civil societies lack any representative mechanisms to reconcile different interests makes their formal involvement in decision-making especially problematic. Unlike governments (which must face elections), and businesses (which must face their shareholders), NGOs have no obvious 'bottom line', and no convenient way to hold themselves accountable. In addition, they usually have a single constituency to satisfy or a single-issue focus, whereas governments must balance competing demands and trade off different interests. However well-intentioned, NGOs are special interest groups and cannot replace a single, strong voice in favour of the common good. It is governments' responsibility to guarantee the universal rights and entitlements of citizens.

Why have NGOs grown so much?

There has been an explosive growth in the number, size and reach of the transnational NGO movement, especially since the end of the Cold War. The 176 'international' NGOs of 1909 had blossomed into 28,900 by 1993, and over 20,000 transnational NGO networks are already active on the world stage, 90 per cent of which were formed during the last thirty years. The story is the same in developing countries, except those with repressive regimes. In Nepal, the number of NGOs registered with government grew from 220 in 1990 to 1,210 in 1993; in Tunisia, from 1,886 in 1988 to 5,186 just three years later. In 1996, the largest ever survey of the non-profit sector found over a million such groups in India, and 210,000 in

Brazil. NGO enthusiasts see this as evidence of a fundamental 'power shift', an 'associational revolution' as profound as the rise of the nation state in the eighteenth century.

This may be premature or just romantic, but the rise of NGOs *is* a significant phenomenon. Something important – and potentially historic – is happening in world politics. NGO action around the World Trade Organisation meeting in Seattle may prove to be a pivotal moment in the evolution of the worldwide NGO movement. Though more a staging post than the 'new dawn' claimed by some, post-Seattle it is no longer possible for governments or businesses to dismiss the claims of NGOs outright, or to pretend that they do not loom large on the political radar screen. The giant multinational Monsanto is the latest to find this out – forced to abandon its controversial 'terminator gene' by a combination of NGO protest and careful pressure by the Rockefeller Foundation in New York.

There are at least three reasons for the rapid rise of NGOs. **The first is that ideas about international development have moved on, away from the notorious 'Washington Consensus'** – the belief that free markets and liberal democracy provided a universal recipe for growth and poverty-reduction. NGOs are no longer simply instruments to pick up the pieces of state and market failure ('ladles in the global soup kitchen' as some have called them), but a force for transformation in global politics and economics. A strong social and institutional infrastructure is now seen as crucial to growth and development: 'social capital' – a rich weave of social networks, norms and civic institutions – is just as important as other forms of capital to these ends. Pluralistic decision-making is seen as more effective in developing a social consensus about structural changes in the economy, and other key reforms: shared ownership of the development agenda is seen as the key to its sustainability. And, as the 'third way' constantly reminds us, public, private and civic roles are being re-conceptualized and reshaped in both economics and social policy: the best route to problem-solving lies through partnership.

Second, involving NGOs is cost-effective public relations, especially for institutions (like the World Bank and the IMF) that are
under attack for their secrecy and weak accountability. James
Wolfensohn has bought priceless support from shareholder governments by opening the doors of the World Bank to Oxfam and
other well-known campaigners on debt, health and education.
International agencies have found that partnerships with NGOs
contribute to more efficient project implementation and a lower
rate of failure; a better public image and more political support,
especially among key shareholder governments in North America
and Western Europe; and research and policy which is more
informed and less constrained by internal orthodoxy. Given these
tangible benefits, it would be difficult to retreat from the trend
towards greater NGO engagement; the practical and political costs
would be too high. There is a less positive side to this story, since
some would claim that NGOs have moved 'too close for comfort' to
the centres of world power. They have been unwitting accomplices
in the drive to retrench the state, privatize government responsibilities, and erode the social contracts that protect the universal
rights of citizens. In the process, NGOs can easily be co-opted and
lose their radical voice – a charge recently levelled by *The
Economist* magazine at NGOs in dialogue with the World Bank.
Nevertheless, the trend toward constructive engagement contin-
ues. Indeed, the refusal of protestors to play by these rules is one
reason for the consternation that has spread through powerful
institutions since the 'battle of Seattle' – 'just when we thought the
water was safe', so to speak, 'the NGO sharks have re-entered the
ocean'.

**Third, what was once unthinkable in international relations is
rapidly becoming accepted: non-state actors have a crucial role to
play in global governance.** Few people now trust governments
alone to represent the views of every interest in society. NGOs
provide additional channels for popular participation, and help to
ensure that those on the margins also have a voice. This is just as
true at the global level, especially when international networks

may provide the only outlet for the citizens of non-democratic regimes. Traditionally, governance has been seen as the preserve of the nation state, but developments that accelerated toward the close of the 20th century may have consigned that notion to the increasingly crowded 'dustbin of history'. Pollution and disease do not respect national sovereignty, and nor do security threats from terrorism, international criminals, ethno-nationalist warfare and drugs. People and capital flow across increasingly porous borders, demanding co-operation between countries to manage investment sensibly and level up working conditions in a world of integrated markets. And co-operative management requires a system of global governance – a set of rules, norms and institutions that govern behaviour across national boundaries. The key word here is 'governance', not 'government', recognizing that business and civil society must share in constructing the regimes of the future, and that while globalisation has changed the terms of contemporary political debate, there is no constituency or prospect of a 'global government'. The age of 'soft power' has arrived, bringing in its wake a gradual but potentially seismic shift in international relations – in which global governance is likely to consist, not of a single framework of international law applied through national state authorities, but of a patchwork quilt of agreements negotiated between governments, corporations and citizens' groups at different levels of the world system.

At a time when governance must contend with increasingly international problems, the authority of states is being challenged by the rising power of private actors, both for-profit and not-for-profit. It is important not to exaggerate these trends, since governments are still capable of regulating both the private sphere and civil society. In any case, "international governance does not mean the end of nations, any more than an orchestra means the end of violins", said the late Prime Minister of Israel, Golda Meir, but if centralised authority is the only instrument we have it will inevitably play to the tune of the already powerful. Pluralistic regimes are the only alternative we have in a climate where global government remains politically unfeasible. The future of global governance lies in a fairer distribution of power through the international system, expressed through a wider variety of channels, and with many more checks and balances.

NGOs are an essential component of these checks and balances. As I have argued elsewhere, the regimes of the future are likely to be composed of a small core of negotiated minimum standards, surrounded by a much larger array of voluntary regulations and other, non-coercive means of influencing destructive behaviour. Take the example of global warming, where a legally-binding regime has proved impossible to agree but other solutions – including tradable emissions permits and industrial clean-up locally – are gradually being put in place through a mixture of government direction, business action, and NGO lobbying. It is the changing balance between 'soft' and 'hard' power, formal and informal politics, that is characteristic of governance in a globalising world. When the Nobel Peace Prize was awarded to the International Campaign to Ban Landmines in 1998, the selection committee expressed their hope that partnership between governments and civil society would become the diplomatic model for the 21st Century.

Prior to 1980, there was little structured contact between NGOs and multilateral institutions, and almost no formal non-state involvement in global regimes. Toward the middle of the 1980s such contacts became more frequent and more organized, including the consolidation of NGO advisory or consultative bodies for the specialized agencies of the UN system, the formation of the NGO Working Group on the World Bank in 1984, and some early global campaigning efforts around debt and structural adjustment. Successive UN conferences on gender, population, the environment, social development and shelter provided a vehicle for these emerging alliances to test out their skills, and both the UN and the World Bank began to form strategic partnerships with key NGOs in ventures such as the Global Alliance for Forest Conservation and Sustainable Use, the World Commission on Dams, and the Marine

Stewardship Council. By the mid-1990s NGO involvement had largely been accepted as a way of creating additional channels for popular participation, accountability, consultation and debate, underpinned by huge improvements in the speed and sophistication of electronic communication that enables citizens across the world to communicate with each other in an instant.

Over the past five years, NGOs have been increasingly effective in using these opportunities to insert the voices of under-represented groups into the global arena. Three types of involvement have become especially important:

- *Changing the language of debates* – for example around debt relief and how to spend the proceeds, where G7 governments have increasingly adopted Jubilee 2000's proposals since a 'human chain' surrounded their Summit meeting in Birmingham in 1998.
- *Negotiating the detail of regimes* – for example the Ottawa land-mines treaty, which was driven through by a global NGO alliance (the International Campaign to Ban Landmines) and a group of middle-power governments, led by Canada.
- *Monitoring and enforcing global agreements* – for example, the implementation of measures to combat child labor in Bangladesh and Pakistan, which were negotiated by NGOs, governments and factory owners and backed up by on-site visits and NGO programs to provide alternative sources of income for the families of child workers.

These openings are significant, but not surprisingly NGOs have stopped short of formal involvement in decision-making, and have been kept away from the most important forums for discussion. For example, NGOs can already attend WTO ministerial conferences and ad hoc symposia on specific subjects, but they (along with developing world governments) are excluded from the 'green room' where the real business of negotiation takes place, and are unable to access key documents unless permitted by their governments. Other international bodies fare little better. The NGO Working Group on the World Bank meets the Bank's Board of Directors once a year for an hour or so, while the various NGO consultative groups in the UN system meet more often, but rarely exchange more than pleasantries and the occasional mild rebuke. So although the rationale for increasing NGO involvement is powerful and persuasive – as a counterweight to the growing power of corporations and the declining authority of states – we lack the concrete mechanisms to turn this logic into reality. The result is a growing democratic deficit in global institutions. Correcting this situation rests on molding an international system in which all countries can be stakeholders (not just their governments) and whose essential fairness is recognised by all. And that requires a more equal voice for developing countries in negotiating global regimes (19 African delegates to the WTO don't even have permanent trade missions in Geneva), and a stronger role for citizens in negotiating the positions of their governments.

As this process proceeds, it is important to remind ourselves that the role of civil society – and especially NGOs – is to fill in the spaces of a healthy democracy and not to substitute for government. One of the defining characteristics of NGOs is that they do not seek state power, even though the boundaries between formal and informal politics will always be somewhat porous, especially in countries where formal citizenship rights are weak. Such multi-layered, pluralistic forms of governance are complex and unpredictable, but over time they should be more effective – by giving ordinary citizens more of a say in the questions that dominate world politics and a greater stake in the solutions.

3. Fall from grace: the problems of NGO involvement

As a result of the political openings of the last decade, NGOs feel they have the *right* to participate in global decision-making. Much less attention has been paid to their *obligations* in pursuing this role responsibly, or to concrete ways in which these rights might be expressed. Facing up to these questions is the need of the hour, but this is sensitive and difficult ground for all involved.

"Luddites", "extremists", "save-the-turtle activists", "the leftover left", "loonies and paranoids." Thus spake *Newsweek, Time* and *The Economist* in the aftermath of the battle for Seattle and the skirmishes it has spawned. It is easy to dismiss the growing criticism of the NGO phenomenon, especially about the role of advocacy NGOs from North America and Western Europe, as special pleading by big business, which already defends its interests in the WTO and elsewhere through well-organised and well-resourced lobby groups that enjoy high level access to official negotiations. For example, US and European corporations already meet regularly to plan their lobbying strategies through the 'Transatlantic Business Dialogue', and the European Commission coordinated throughout 1999 with an 'Investment Network' of 60 leading corporations on priorities for a new investment agreement in the WTO.

But the criticism goes deeper than this. In private meetings with government officials, American trade unions are challenging the right of NGOs to occupy such a prominent place in policy debates, and old assumptions about NGO strengths – like closeness to the poor, high levels of innovation, and cost-effectiveness – are being challenged by a growing body of research. Large numbers of new NGOs have sprung up, especially in developing countries, but many are entirely dependent on foreign aid for their existence and represent little more than a computer, a project proposal, and an aspiring entrepreneur. "If your son is looking for a good marriage, make sure he has an NGO to include in the dowry for his wife" as a new joke runs in Pakistan. In short, the rosy-tinted spectacles are well and truly off, and criticising NGOs has become a favourite pastime of academics, politicians, and the press. It is not that the principle of civic engagement is being questioned by these critics; more that the practice of civic engagement can be distorted in favor of organizations with greater resources and more access to decision-makers. Current trends in the United Nations system illustrate this ambiguity of commitment: strong declarations from the Secretary-General and others about the importance of civil society, accompanied by increasing attempts to formalize – some would say restrict – access by NGOs to the machinery of debate and decision making, especially in New York. At the beginning of the 21st Century there are forces acting both for and against greater NGO involvement in global governance. This chapter seeks to outline the grounds for criticism, to assess how far the critics are justified, and to look for constructive ways in which NGOs can answer the questions that are being posed about them.

a) Problems of legitimacy – why should we listen to NGOs?

The first set of issues – and by far the most contentious – concern questions of legitimacy. Who – if anyone – do NGOs represent, or are they just unaccountable special interest groups that wear a more friendly disguise? Who enjoys the benefits and suffers the costs of what the movement achieves, especially at the grassroots level? Who speaks for whom in an NGO alliance, and how are differences resolved when participants vary in strength and resources? Whose voice is heard, and which interests are ignored, when differences are filtered out in order to communicate a simple message? In particular, how are grassroots voices mediated by institutions of different kinds – networks and their members, Northern NGOs and Southern NGOs, Southern NGOs and community groups, and so on down the line? These questions touch the rawest of NGO raw nerves, but they will not go away.

When problems surface in this area, they usually centre on three problems: transparency, accountability, and accuracy.

Transparency: when NGOs claim to 'represent' the poor, they are rarely specific about which poor people they are representing, or how. Actually, most NGOs are more sophisticated than this and accept that their policy positions are their own, even if substantial consultation has taken place with 'partners' in the South. But a lack of transparency about who is really speaking, combined with the extreme asymmetry of global networks, makes NGOs easy targets for criticism on these grounds. For example, only 251 of the 1,550 NGOs associated with the UN Department of Public Information come from the South, and the ratio of NGOs in consultative status with ECOSOC is even lower. Are NGO campaigns a disguise for Northern interests, a more subtle form of colonialism, however well-intentioned? Even something as innocuous as Oxfam's education campaign has been upbraided for its focus on Western models of formal schooling, so often criticized by sociologists for reproducing inequality. In the mid-1990s, North American NGOs claimed to represent a Southern consensus against replenishment of the International Development Association (the soft loan arm of the World Bank), on the grounds that social and environmental safeguards were too weak. In contrast, Southern NGOs (mainly from Africa) insisted that IDA go ahead regardless of these weaknesses, since foreign aid was desperately required. On some issues (like debt or landmines), there is a solid South-North consensus in favor of a unified lobbying position. However, in other areas (especially trade and labor rights, and the environment), there is no such consensus, since people may have conflicting short-term interests in different parts of the world. As globalization proceeds, these areas will become the centerpiece of the international system's response, so it is vital that NGO networks develop a more sophisticated way of acknowledging and addressing differences of opinion within civil society in different localities and regions.

Accountability: NGO accountability is weak and problematic, since there is no clear 'bottom line' for results and no single authority to which NGOs must report on their activities. Where transparency is poor and networks are dominated by voices from the North, accountability to the grassroots is likely to be weak, but this is far from a theoretical question. What if the NGOs who protested so loudly in Seattle turn out to be wrong in their assumptions about the future benefits that flow from different trading strategies – who pays the price? Not the NGOs themselves, but farmers in the Third World who have never heard of Christian Aid or Save the Children, but who will suffer the consequences for generations. The same strictures apply to pro free-traders too of course, but NGOs cannot use this as a defence. The recent 'banana wars' provide another example of this problem, where NGOs supporting small-scale banana producers in Central America and the Caribbean found themselves on opposite sides of a landmark dispute before the World Trade Organisation. Because they form a small part of a much broader civil society, NGOs cannot represent the voice of citizen action, and global NGO networks must be carefully scrutinised to establish whose interests are driving the agenda. Dealing with these differences requires accountability mechanisms 'downwards' (to the poor) as well as 'upwards' to the donors who fund the NGO's activities. This is a challenge that no NGO has addressed.

Accuracy: NGO positions are often criticised as crude and simplistic, poorly researched, and driven by fashion and sensation rather than loyalty to the facts, or to any public constituency. This makes them easy targets for their critics to lampoon, or (at their most charitable) write off as well-meaning people who are hopelessly ill informed about the ways of the world (i.e. the ways of *The Economist*). In fact, many NGOs have substantial research departments, and Oxfam's critiques are even cited by the IMF. Nevertheless, there is always a temptation in NGO campaigns to trade off rigor for speed and profile. The Brent Spar oil rig controversy is a good example, where Greenpeace overestimated by a factor of 37 the amount of hydrocarbons that might leak into the surrounding ocean. NGO attacks against the World Bank and the IMF (Oxfam's excepted) are often similarly misplaced, not because these institutions are perfect (far from it), but because it is difficult to imagine an attack on global poverty that doesn't involve an efficient lender of last resort, and a ready supply of subsidised development finance. The absence of more thoughtful critiques also gives unwitting support to isolationism and protectionist forces, especially in North America, who care little about what happens in the developing world. The challenge lies in building the analytical capacity of NGOs without pretending that they can be universities or think-tanks.

Underlying all three problems is the thorny issue of legitimacy. Legitimacy is generally understood as the right to be and do something in society – a sense that an organization is lawful, admissible and justified in its chosen course of action – but there are different ways to validate these things: through representation (which usually confers the right to participate in decision making), and through effectiveness (which only confers the right to be heard). Legitimacy in membership bodies is claimed through the normal democratic processes of elections and formal sanctions that ensure that an agency is representative of, and accountable to, its constituents. Trade unions and some NGOs fall into this category, though whether these processes operate effectively and democratically is another matter – agreeing on some minimum standards in this regard is an important part of the agenda for the future.

By contrast, non-membership NGOs define their legitimacy according to legal compliance, effective oversight by their trustees, and recognition by other legitimate bodies that they have valuable knowledge and skills to bring to the table. No one expects Oxfam, for example, to be perfectly representative of developing world opinion; only that its proposals on debt and other issues should be solidly rooted in research and experience, and sensitive to the views and aspirations of its Southern partners. So most NGOs have a legitimate right to a voice, but not to a vote, in global affairs. In this sense, the best representative of civil society is a democratically elected government, complemented by the checks and balances provided by non-state membership bodies (such as labor unions), and pressure groups of different kinds. The resulting mix is often messy, but it is standard practice in national politics and looks set to shape the emergence of more democratic regimes at the global level too. Transnational civil society is far from democratic, and few networks have democratic systems of governance and accountability. Nevertheless, the increasing voice of NGOs adds an essential layer of checks and balances into the international system, and helps to ensure that excluded views are heard. The challenge is to structure global citizen voice in ways that combat, rather than accentuate, existing social, economic and political inequalities.

Early efforts that have tried to do this have used certification and self-regulation to ensure that NGOs are practicing what they preach. Formal accreditation already exists in many United Nations bodies and has been used by bodies such as CONGO (the 'Conference of NGOs in Consultative Relationship with the United Nations') to structure NGO participation in the follow-up to the Rio, Beijing and Copenhagen global conferences. The UN has a range of categories for NGOs including general consultative status (for large NGOs whose work covers most areas of the UN's activities), special consultative status (for NGOs with specific competence in a given field), and roster status (for NGOs that make occasional contributions). Each category conveys a different set of rights of access to UN documents, observer status at the General Assembly, and the right to submit written statements and place items on an agenda. To be eligible, NGOs must meet criteria set out by the UN, including a democratically adopted constitution, a representative structure (transparent decision-making or formal voting), evidence that they derive most of their resources from national affiliates or members, and a description of their finances and activities. The WTO has adopted a limited version of this approach, and APEC uses a variant called 'legitimacy determinants' which provide a way of selecting NGOs on the basis of the degree of 'helpful knowledge' they bring to the discussions.

The most sophisticated example of self-regulation at the global level is the NGO Steering committee of the UN Commission on Sustainable Development, which has developed a detailed set of guidelines covering membership and decision-making that help to build its legitimacy in the eyes of both governments and business. This has turned out to be quite bureaucratic, with regional and sector-based caucuses, detailed electoral procedures, and sanctions for those found guilty of breaking the rules – almost as if the NGOs are competing to replicate the mind-numbing minutiae of their official UN counterparts. These rules can also be used by governments to frustrate NGO involvement through filibustering and delaying tactics. Partly as a result of these problems, other NGOs have criticised the committee for becoming a gatekeeper instead of a bridge. Nevertheless, this is an experiment that deserves serious attention, and one that is already being followed up through multistakeholder dialogues in other UN forums. One reason for its success is the fact that NGOs sit alongside representatives from trade unions and business as equal partners.

It is no accident that questions about legitimacy are being raised at a time when NGOs have started to gain real influence on the international stage. In that sense they are victims of their own success. Neither is there any shortage of hypocrisy among the critics, especially when it appears that NGOs are being singled out in contrast to businesses (and even many governments) that are even less accountable than they are. Nevertheless, the criticisms are real, and must be addressed if NGOs are to exploit the political space that has opened up in the post Cold-War world. At the minimum, that means no more unsubstantiated claims to 'represent the people', and an explicit recognition that voice and vote require different ways of claiming organizational legitimacy and maintaining it over time.

b) Problems of disconnection – are global NGOs in touch with local communities?

Globalisation requires both governments and NGOs to link different levels of their activity together – local, national, regional and global. For governments this task is somewhat more straightforward, since they have a chain of inter-governmental structures like the United Nations through which debate and decision-making can be linked, at least in theory. The situation is much more challenging for NGOs, since there are no formal structures to facilitate supra-national civic participation. As a result, NGO advocacy on the global stage is often weakly rooted in local and national debates, and dominated by voices from North America and Western Europe.

The outcome is that NGOs find it difficult to build their policy platforms democratically, and end up by circumventing the political processes that could supply some answers to the criticisms of legitimacy explored above. These problems are not helped by a tendency among some NGOs to focus on global advocacy to the exclusion of the national-level processes of state-society relations that underpin the ability of any country to pursue progressive goals in an integrated economy. There is always a temptation to 'leap-frog' over the national arena and go direct to Washington or Brussels, where it is often easier to gain access to senior officials, and achieve a response. This is understandable, but in the long term it is a serious mistake. It increases the influence of multilateral institutions over national development and erodes the process of domestic coalition building that is essential to the development of pro-poor policy reform. In addition, the constant appearance of NGOs in international forums, combined with the dominance of NGO voices from the North, reinforces the suspicion among developing world governments that these are not genuine global alliances but yet another example of the rich world's monopoly over global debates. The NGOs concerned may see themselves as defending the interests of the poor, but it is still outsiders – not the government's own constituents – who are deciding the agenda. There is a danger that the high profile and accessibility of global protests will detract from the real business of local politics, where participation is much more meaningful and NGOs can add real value to building a democratic national consensus on each society's response to globalisation.

Addressing this problem requires a different way of building NGO alliances, with more emphasis on horizontal relationships among equals; stronger links between local, national and global action; and a more democratic way of deciding on strategy and messages. Jubilee 2000 (though a relatively easy case because of the absence of any South-North fault-line) provides some good examples of these innovations. In Uganda for example, local NGOs developed a dialogue with their own government on the options for debt relief, supported by technical assistance from Northern NGOs like Oxfam. The results of this dialogue were then incorporated into the international debt campaign. 'Rede Bancos' played a similar role in Brazil. Or take the example of NGOs in Costa Rica which are performing 'social audits' of banana plantations using international standards reinterpreted to suit local conditions, with advice from global NGO campaigners.

These experiments are the local building blocks of future global governance. By laying a strong foundation for negotiations over labor standards, environmental pollution and human rights, they offer the potential to connect ordinary citizens to global regimes. But this can only work if local structures are connected to more democratic structures at higher levels of the world system, which can ensure that sacrifices made in one locality are not exploited by less scrupulous counterparts elsewhere. Recent tripartite agreements on child labor in Bangladeshi garment factories are a sign of the future in this respect, with NGOs, government and business striking mutually advantageous local bargains within a framework of global minimum standards set out in the provisions of the ILO Convention. The 'National Councils for Sustainable Development' that have grown up in many Asian countries represent another way in which 'top-down meets bottom-up' in global environmental regulation. Other regimes could follow these examples by embedding local agreements in a nested system of authorities that balance necessary flexibility with a core of universal principles. Getting things right at the base of the system – by generating a strong local consensus about policy positions – is much more important than 'building castles in the sky' – new global institutions divorced from any local roots.

These innovations show that NGO networks can achieve their policy goals, build capacity among NGOs in the South, encourage partnerships with Southern governments, *and* preserve accountability to grassroots constituents, if they consciously plan to do so from the outset and are prepared to trade-off some element of speed and convenience in order to negotiate a more democratic set of outcomes. Sadly, too few Northern NGOs seem willing to follow this approach. Perhaps the costs seem too high, in terms of profile foregone and decision-making made more complex. As we shall see, Northern governments can help NGOs to deal with these costs and encourage them to make the transition to alliances that are constructed from the bottom up.

c) Problems of short-termism: why campaign slogans don't build constituencies for change.

One of the consequences of globalization is that traditional answers to social and economic questions become redundant, or at least that the questions become more complex and the answers more uncertain. The theoretical underpinnings of pro- and anti free-trade positions, for example, are highly contested, yet NGOs are famous for their advocacy in favour of predetermined positions. These positions are often couched in terms of strong opposition to the status quo, yet by itself a politics of protest is unlikely to yield many of the answers to complex social and economic problems. "We know what we don't like, but we don't know what might work better" could be the mantra of the NGO community. Humility doesn't come easy to organisations that have been used to occupying the moral high ground. In this situation, more investment in research and learning is crucial so that NGO alternatives can be properly-grounded, tested and critiqued. Another requirement is to switch from 'conversion' strategies (the traditional NGO view of advocacy) to 'engagement', which aims to support a process of dialogue rather than simply lobbying for a fixed set of outcomes. This will take NGOs further into territory that may seem obvious ground for them – building public constituencies for policy reform in the rich world – but which has been largely absent from their agenda.

A strong constituency in industrialised countries is a pre-requisite for the success of more equitable global regimes, new forms of governance, and the sacrifices required to alter global patterns of consumption and trade. Codes of conduct to govern multi-national corporations, for example, are of little use unless they are backed by large-scale consumer pressure to enforce them. The emphasis here is on changing the public context in which policy-makers work, rather than in seeking to influence negotiations directly, where NGO involvement will always be bedeviled by questions of legitimacy and representation. Although governments and business can play an important role in building these constituencies, the major responsibility is likely to fall to NGOs, since it is they who have the public trust and international connections to talk plainly and convincingly about matters of global justice. NGOs in the UK have always talked of the need to build constituencies, but have focused on problems in the developing world instead of lifestyle change at home, playing on the line that 'your five pounds will make the difference.' It rarely does, and what would make a difference (like mass-based public protest against Western indifference) – is never given sufficient attention. Many NGOs have cut back their public education budgets in recent years (seeing this an overhead rather than a core program), while government spending is only slowly re-surfacing as a result of the White Paper on International Development issued in 1997. Countries that spend properly on international education have already secured a strong base of public support for global co-operation: the Dutch Government spent more than $17 million in 1997 and Sweden $15 million, compared to $3.9 million in the USA and a paltry $1.2 million in Japan.

Engaging more deeply in constituency building doesn't mean abandoning campaigns or surrendering the power of protest, but it does mean a better balance between traditional forms of NGO advocacy and slower, longer-term work on the causes of injustice. Sinking more roots into their own societies would also help NGOs to gain more legitimacy when they move to the international stage. To do this they would have to treat the public as citizens instead of donors, and reach beyond the middle classes that form their traditional supporter base. One of the problems with Global Exchange's campaign against NIKE, for example, has been its lack of support from communities of colour in the USA who identify so closely with NIKE's products and their sponsor, basketball hero Michael Jordan. To support this shift, NGOs will need to develop new skills and competencies in public communications, and work with academics, think-tanks, trade unions and others who can help them to develop and articulate more nuanced positions on issues like trade and labour markets, adapted to different country contexts.

4. Conclusion:
a new deal for global governance

Global governance isn't working. As the world becomes more glob-alised, our global institutions seem to have less and less legitima-cy. And efforts to create the new cooperative structures that we need to tackle global problems and win public support are being hampered by a debate increasingly focused on whether govern-ments, international bureaucracies, big business or interest groups are to blame for the impasse that we face.

More democracy in global governance is the key to a peaceful and prosperous international order – but such regimes are legiti-mate only to the extent that they are grounded in the practice of equal voice and representation. NGOs may consider this an obvious and uncontroversial conclusion – something they have been advocating for years – but as this report has shown such a vision is just as much a challenge to NGOs themselves. In order to claim their seat at the global negotiating table, they must put their own house in order and answer the growing chorus of their critics.

Getting the right role for NGOs in global governance is just one (but important) part of the broader debate about making interna-tional cooperation more effective. And NGOs should not, as a general principle, be held to higher standards of behaviour than any other institution. NGOs may misbehave, of course, but the consequences are rarely as harmful as that of an autocratic government or an unaccountable corporation. But – even if the misuse of NGO power is more an inconvenience to democracy than a fundamental threat – it is important to tackle the issues that threaten to erode the legitimacy of global citizen action. Even soft power has to be disciplined if it is not to be ignored, dismissed or actively repressed by governments along the way. We urgently need to move out of a phase of mutual mistrust and the allocation of blame, to look instead at how NGOs, governments, international organisations and others can work together to improve international cooperation and the results it can deliver.

The best way to do this is not through the heavy hand of bureaucratic regulation, but by encouraging NGOs to put their house in order. Improvements in practice should be rewarded with an institutionalised voice in global debates. These measures need to be 'light but firm' – encouraging improvements in NGO practice without eroding independence or intruding overmuch on the freedom of NGOs to pursue their different agendas, since freedom and diversity are the hallmarks of a healthy civil society. **Three principles for a new deal in global governance** were outlined at the beginning of this report: **what would they actually mean in practice?**

a) A voice not a vote

Since NGOs are not elected and civil societies lack any democratic means of negotiating the vast range of different interests involved, we are unlikely to see a satisfactory 'representative' of civil society sitting on the World Bank's Board or in the UN General Assembly. Much more likely is greater NGO involvement in the informal political process – but with more checks and balances to ensure that everyone's voice is heard. This principle – a voice not a vote, structured to give every interest in civil society a fair and equal hearing – is crucial to resolving the tensions that have emerged over NGOs and their role. Governments and NGOs should agree to open global regimes and institutions to structured

NGO participation, in return for commitments on standards of integrity and special help to those left out of the debate. There are already models of this sort at domestic level, such as the 'Compact on Relations between Government and the Voluntary Sector' in the UK, which has generated improvements on both sides in terms of trust, dialogue and cooperation even though it is not legally binding. The UN Secretariat could pilot the design of such a compact for the Millennium General Assembly later this year, and if it works, follow that up with similar experiments at the World Trade Organization, the IMF and the World Bank. The next three suggestions show how these compacts could be constructed, and what they might mean in practice in selected global institutions.

b) Certification and self-regulation

Structuring the participation of NGOs will require a set of selection criteria and a mechanism for their enforcement. The best way to monitor the required standards of NGO integrity will be largely through **self-regulation,** with the possibility of independent verification or arbitration where necessary. In the Philippines, NGOs already have a code of conduct that is monitored by a semi-independent umbrella body, the 'Philippine Council for NGO Certification', that can recommend withdrawal of registration and tax privileges from NGOs who fail to comply. At the international level this is obviously more difficult, but the example of the Commission on Sustainable Development cited earlier shows that is possible. The first criterion for participation would be certification by the relevant national body, as in the Philippines case. The second would be that each NGO signs up to the standards required by the relevant international network on transparency, accountability, internal democracy and 'helpful knowledge' – the degree of expertise it brings to the table. Disputes over membership or other matters could be dealt with using the network's own complaints procedures and sanctions, or referred to the office of **an independent NGO ombudsman** or 'quality assurance board' located in the UN Secretariat, or the Economic and Social Council. As in other areas of global governance, it will be the UN's role to set and monitor the standards for NGO involvement across all international institutions, and to keep track of the large number of different codes of conduct and structures for participation that will probably evolve.

c) Levelling the playing field

Of course, some NGOs won't want to join these codes of conduct, and will pursue their activities through other channels – good for them, so long as they recognise that certain avenues for influence will therefore be unavailable. Others – especially smaller NGOs and those from the South – will want extra help to enable them to fulfill the standards required. And while governments cannot force NGOs to adhere to rules and regulations in the global arena, they can and should help to level the playing field by equalizing the entry conditions. That means **additional support for Southern NGO participation**, using foreign aid budgets to strengthen their capacity for research and policy analysis ('summer schools' on economic literacy, for example), promote financial independence and sustainability, pay for Southern voices to represent themselves directly in global debates, and reward NGO networks that are more balanced and democratic in their composition.

ALOP (an important Latin American NGO Network) already has its own office in Brussels to lobby the European Union, but this is unusual because Southern networks find it very difficult to raise funds for offices in the North. These are obvious candidates for funds like the Department of International Development's new 'Civil Society Challenge Fund', but resources should be channeled direct to NGOs and networks in the South wherever feasible, rather than through Northern NGO intermediaries. There will be projects where a North-South project partnership will be most effective, but **a strong Southern steer in the overall allocation of resources should be pursued**, perhaps by setting a maximum 25 per cent cap on the amount of the fund that can be channelled through Northern NGOs.

Northern governments can also use their position in international institutions to press for greater access by Southern NGOs to national government delegations, and to encourage Northern NGOs to pay more attention to constituency-building by matching their resources with an equal amount from the UK aid budget. **DFID should double government spending on international education over the next five years** in order to kick-start a new phase of education for international co-operation, **and require all NGOs in receipt of public funds to earmark a minimum proportion of their voluntary income for constituency-building activities.**

d) A structured voice for NGOs in global governance

Once certified and supported by the appropriate resources and capacity-building activities, where would such discussions actually take place? It has been suggested that parallel, non-voting 'civil society chambers' may be the best answer – standing alongside the UN General Assembly, the WTO and the Boards of the World Bank and the IMF. I believe that this could provide a useful and important step forward – but only if we think clearly about how these bodies should work in practice. In each case, the goal should be not just to widen participation but to make each institution more effective in fulfilling its mandate.

Rather than creating a template to be replicated in international organisations across the board, I believe that innovation in global governance could best be fostered from a period of structured experimentation in NGO involvement. Institutions that deal with peacekeeping, development and international financial stability will obviously work with civil society in different ways. We do not yet know what value civil society actors will add in different circumstances, what the drawbacks of different methods of involvement might be, or what unintended consequences may arise. Therefore, a range of different methods should be tried to see which best enable the voices of all to be heard. These might include elections and selections from regional umbrella bodies or national NGO platforms of action. Such regional structures have already proven themselves in relation to NGO lobbying on trade agreements such as NAFTA and MERCOSUR, offering a way to build policy positions from the bottom up while respecting national differences.

The **International Monetary Fund** currently allows no formal participation by civil society groups in debate and decision-making. Given its role as lender of last resort, the market-sensitivity of its decisions and the speed with which they need to be taken, there is unlikely to be a workable scheme of prior consultation with civil society. But by holding a **World Financial Forum** every five years, the IMF could engage civil society actors in broader debate about financial policy, bringing together key stakeholders to assess the evidence of particular interventions once the dust has settled to learn the lessons for its lending policies in the future. One key issue could be how the IMF could better tailor its advice to different circumstances – a major criticism of Fund policy to date: for example, the Asian financial crises had very different causes to those in Russia or Latin America, and the IMF's austerity programmes risked exacerbating recession by applying a standard formula.

The **World Bank** has made much of its greater openness to civil society inputs since the arrival of James Wolfensohn as President. Actual performance in the field still varies considerably, with too much autonomy given to Country and Sector Directors in deciding how to operationalise civil society involvement in the design of Country Assistance Strategies, economic and social research, and the formulation of policy. The result is a patchwork quilt of performance – good, bad and indifferent – but at least the principle of civic participation has been accepted, and is now enshrined in efforts like the 'Comprehensive Development Framework' that aim to improve the coherence and effectiveness of foreign aid. The next step should involve giving relevant NGOs and other civil society groups **the right to monitor the Bank's new Poverty Reduction Strategy Papers**, country by country, with the NGOs seeking to ensure that both the negotiation and the implementation of these strategies draws as much as possible on local knowledge and is as broadly-based and rooted in the host society as possible.

Progress should be assessed through **systematic monitoring of quality standards for NGO participation by a joint World Bank-NGO team** that would report directly to the Bank's Board of Directors every three years.

Feelings of exclusion from the **World Trade Organisation's** processes and procedures – within the conference hall as well as on the streets outside – contributed to the Seattle meetings' failure to achieve its goals. Southern-based NGOs can rightly claim that the vast imbalance of NGO representation skewed the civil society debate around Seattle towards Northern concerns – but developing-country governments, especially new members of the WTO, also faced major, sometimes unaffordable, costs to attend or prepare for the meetings and to find out how they worked when they got there. If access and participation are to be increased, it is vital that questions of capacity-building for governments and NGOs are tackled together. **Member governments should create a WTO participation fund** to tackle these capacity-building issues. The fund should be used to ensure that all developing country members are able to be represented at future summit meetings; it should provide funds to enable civil society actors to be included in government delegations for governments who want to take up this option, and it should find ways to build the necessary economic and legal literacy for meaningful NGO participation through workshops, mentoring and other training schemes. The legitimacy of the WTO would also be enhanced by ensuring that it is as open and transparent as possible in its decision-making procedures. Key civil society stakeholders with a material interest in trade disputes should be given **access to individual dispute-resolution negotiations**, and provision should be made for civil society involvement in a **multi-stakeholder review of the outcomes of disputes every three years.**

A period of experimentation will enable global governance institutions, governments and NGOs to learn, not just from their own experiences but from the comparative lessons learned across the board. It should also help to build the effectiveness and legitimacy of global bodies, and strengthen public support for them. For example, greater engagement with civil society would give the IMF a forum to communicate its activities at a time when there is growing grassroots criticism of financial institutions in general, and an increasing body of opinion, for example on the US right, that opposes the very idea of a lender of last resort. Offering concrete support to enable poorer countries and NGOs to participate would strengthen the WTO's claims to be creating a fair and open rules-based trading regime.

e) A safe space for dialogue

These suggestions aim to be 'light but firm' – encouraging innovations and improvements in NGO practice without eroding independence or intruding overmuch on the freedom of NGOs to pursue their different agendas. Nevertheless they are likely to be controversial, and will certainly be difficult to translate into concrete actions. NGOs, governments and business need a 'safe space' in which to talk about these dilemmas, free from the accusations, anecdotes, prejudice and confusion that dominate the current debate. The UK Government should volunteer to host and pay for these discussions in the form of a **'Forum for Global Governance', to be held in London in the aftermath of the Millennium General Assembly.** The mechanisms for NGO representation laid out above could be piloted in the organisation of this event, and NGOs and governments encouraged to prepare position papers on innovative solutions – not more general rhetoric. Over time, the aim should be for these discussions to develop into a basic guide to the 'rules of the game' for NGO participation in global regimes, to be adopted by governments and international organisations across the world and monitored by the UN Secretariat.

Changing the rules of the game

Over the last ten years, NGOs have pushed consistently for greater fairness in the rules of the globalisation game – fair trade and investment, and equal participation in molding the regimes of the future. Though stereotyped as 'Luddites', most NGOs are not against globalisation as such, merely advocates for global democracy and human rights as well as market integration. Translating these principles into detailed policy prescriptions has proven difficult for NGOs – as well as for governments – but in helping to enshrine them as a new bottom line in international affairs, NGOs have already changed the terms of the globalisation debate forever.

Whether they are more or less 'representative', and right or wrong on the fine print of their critiques, are not the most important questions, since NGOs differ so much on these questions even among themselves. But principles of equal voice and representation are things that all NGOs can agree on, whether lobbyists or service-providers, radical or reformist, from the South or from the North.

The suggestions made in this report will not solve all of the problems of NGO participation, but they should help to assuage the criticisms that threaten to turn back the tide of global citizen action. This is an important point, because – despite the problems, the gaps and the weaknesses – the increasing involvement of NGOs in global governance has been a significant force for good. The land mines campaign, Jubilee 2000, the women's and environmental movements and many others have secured real advances for people on the margins of global progress. NGOs are rarely angelic in their behavior, but generally speaking they are on the side of the angels, and the world is a better place for them. At the start of a new century, NGOs and governments have reached an historic moment in their relationship with each other. The old antagonisms have largely disappeared, to be replaced by a more complex picture in which there are no easy answers and few issues that generate an immediate consensus. Greater openness to NGO involvement brings more responsibility to play that role effectively, sensitively, and in ways which genuinely give voice to the poor. This is a challenge to all NGOs, and to all governments. We must all be supportive of efforts to grapple with this new agenda, and committed to meeting our side of the bargain in opening the regimes of the future to global citizen action.

Also available from The Foreign Policy Centre

Individual publications should be ordered from Central Books, 99 Wallis Road, London, E9 5LN tel: 020 8986 5488, fax: 020 8533 5821 email: mo@centralbooks.com

THE FOREIGN POLICY CENTRE MISSION STATEMENT
March 3rd 1999; Free, with £1 p+p, or free with any pamphlet.

'Likely to be controversial with Mandarins and influential with Ministers' **Financial Times**

RE-ENGAGING RUSSIA
John Lloyd, journalist and member of The Foreign Policy Centre's advisory council March 2000; £9.95, plus £1 p+p. ISBN 0-9535598-6-6

Published in association with BP Amoco

'Re-engaging Russia is excellent on where Russia's relationships with the west went wrong … thought-provoking, highly-enjoyable, creative and timely' **Keith Vaz, Minister for Europe**

'Characteristically thoughtful and well-written, the pamphlet by this outstanding journalist and Russia-watcher recognises the failures both of post-Soviet Russia and of western policy towards that country. John Lloyd argues convincingly that the answer is not for the west to disengage in Russia but to engage differently' **Professor Archie Brown, St Antony's College Oxford**

AFTER MULTICULTURALISM
Yasmin Alibhai-Brown, The Foreign Policy Centre May 2000; £9.95 plus £1 p+p. ISBN 0-9535598-8-2

Yasmin Alibhai-Brown argues that we need to fundamentally rethink our approach to national identity, race and public culture. The old debate about multiculturalism no longer illuminates the new challenges for reinventing identity and participation in a devolved Britain, a plural Europe and an increasingly interdependent world. We need to leave behind a debate about 'ethnic minorities', which has too often only engaged blacks and asians rather than whites as well, if the coming battles over political culture and national identity are to have a progressive outcome.

NETWORK EUROPE

Mark Leonard, The Foreign Policy Centre
September 1999; £9.95, plus £1 p+p. ISBN 0-9535598-2-3
Published in association with Clifford Chance

A radical new agenda for European reform, arguing that pro-Europeans must reshape the European debate if Europe is to be both effective and popular. Instead of the traditional federalist reform agenda, the EU should learn from successful network models of business organisation and introduce elements of direct democracy to reconnect to its citizens.

'A welcome contribution to the important debate about Europe's future' **Rt Hon Tony Blair MP, Prime Minister**

'A radical agenda for reform from the government's favourite foreign policy think-tank' **Stephen Castle, Independent on Sunday**

NEW VISIONS FOR EUROPE: The Millennium Pledge

Mark Leonard, Vidhya Alakeson and Stephen Edwards, The Foreign Policy Centre
November 1999; £2.95, plus £1 p+p ISBN 0-9535598-5-8
Published in association with Clifford Chance

A proposed commitment from the governments to the peoples of Europe, outlining the approach and policy reforms which could help to reconnect the EU to its citizens.

HOW TO WIN THE EURO REFERENDUM: Lessons from 1975

Robert M. Worcester, Chairman, MORI International
5th June 2000 £9.95, plus £1 p+p. ISBN 0-9535598-6-6

Twenty-five years ago, the British public voted 'Yes' to Europe. Yet the pro-European coalition had to turn around hostile public opinion to win a decisive two-to-one victory in the June 1975 referendum. Today, whether Britain joins the Euro will be one of the defining political issues of this decade - and again, the anti-Europeans are making the running. Can history repeat itself, or will the Eurosceptics have their day at last? Bob Worcester looks at the factors which were decisive in the 1975 referendum, and examines the lessons which we can learn for the Europe debate today.

GOING PUBLIC: DIPLOMACY FOR THE INFORMATION SOCIETY

Mark Leonard and Vidhya Alakeson, The Foreign Policy Centre
May 2000; £9.95 plus £1 p+p. ISBN 0-9535598-7-4
The project is supported by the BBC World Service, The British Council, and the Design Council.

In an age of global communications, building links with overseas publics will matter as much to foreign policy as talking to governments. Whether Britain wants a lasting coalition for international action in Kosovo, the French to lift the beef ban or Russia to become a stable democracy, influencing people abroad must be central to our strategy. The usual diplomatic channels can't do this on their own. The Foreign Office must unleash the energy of 60 million budding ambassadors in Britain's schools, businesses, local authorities, political parties and communities to build deeper links across the world. Going Public shows how global transformations in security, sovereignty and economics mean that diplomats must deal with a new global society where power and influence depend as much on values and reputation as on military might. Going Public shows how Britain should fuse the strengths of traditional and public diplomacy to build the relationships we need to thrive in a globalised world.

MAKING THE COMMONWEALTH MATTER – Interim Report

Kate Ford and Sunder Katwala, The Foreign Policy Centre
April 1999; £4.95, plus £1 p+p. ISBN 0-9535598-1-5

*'The biggest shake-up of the Commonwealth since it was set up in its present form 50 years ago' **The Independent on Sunday***

TRADING IDENTITIES: Why countries and companies are taking on each others' roles

Wally Olins, co-founder of Wolff Olins, branding and identity consultant.
October 1999, £9.95, plus £1 p+p ISBN 0-9535598-3-1

Countries and companies are changing fast – and they are becoming more like each other. As countries develop their 'national brands' to compete for investment, trade and tourism, mega-merged global companies are using nation-building techniques to achieve internal cohesion across cultures and are becoming ever more involved in providing public services like education and health. Wally Olins asks what these cross-cutting trends mean for the new balance of global power.

*'a fascinating pamphlet', **Peter Preston, The Guardian***

40   The Foreign Policy Centre

REINVENTING THE COMMONWEALTH

Kate Ford and Sunder Katwala, The Foreign Policy Centre
November 1999; £9.95, plus £1 p+p. ISBN 0-9535598-4-5

Published in association with the Royal Commonwealth Society

Launched at the Durban Heads of Government Meeting, this report shows how wide-ranging Commonwealth reform could create a modern, effective and relevant organisation - helping members to thrive in the 21st century by creating an internationally-recognised standard for good governance and the conditions for investment.

'Wide-reaching and intelligent' **The Times**

GLOBALIZATION – KEY CONCEPTS, NUMBER ONE

David Held & Anthony McGrew, David Goldblatt & Jonathan Perraton
April 1999; £4.95, plus £1 p+p. ISBN 0-9535598-0-7

Globalization is the buzz-word of the age – but how many people understand it? In this much-needed concise and authoritative guide, globalization's leading theorists thrash out what it really means, and argue that we need to rethink politics to keep up with the changing shape of power. Globalization launches the Key Concepts series – holding all of the hidden assumptions behind foreign policy up to the light, and unpacking the key terms to find out what they really mean for policy-makers today.

'An indispensable counterweight to optimists and pessimists alike'
Will Hutton

Forthcoming publications

THE POST-MODERN STATE AND THE NEW WORLD ORDER
Robert Cooper, Cabinet Office (writing in a personal capacity)
2nd edition. Published in association with Demos.

What did 1989 really mean? Robert Cooper argues that the end of the Cold War also marked the end of the balance-of-power system in Europe. Yet today's open, multilateral post-modern states must deal with a complex world – where many states follow traditional realpolitik, while collapsed and failing states present the dangers of pre-modern chaos. The second edition of this groundbreaking pamphlet also addresses how the role of religion in international politics is very different today.

(prov) RETHINKING SOVEREIGNTY
David Held, Professor of Politics and Sociology, Open University

What does sovereignty mean today, when the collective fortunes of peoples are increasingly intertwined? David Held examines how changes in security, economics, communications and political activism are reshaping ideas of political community. How should democracy and politics keep up with the changing shape of power?

MODERNISING ISLAM
Ziauddin Sardar, writer and broadcaster

This timely, controversial and challenging report argues that the Muslim diaspora, far from being a threat and mere agents of a global Islamic fundamentalist agenda, can play a positive role in updating Islam.

DEMOCRATISING GLOBAL SPORT
Sunder Katwala, The Foreign Policy Centre

Sporting scandals – from match-fixing in cricket and drugs at the tour de France, to cities buying votes to host the Olympics and illegal 'bungs' in football transfers – have shaken many major sports to their foundations. This report will address how the governance of international sport can cope with an age of globalization, commercialisation and accountability – proposing reforms to better reconcile the interests of athletes, supporters, sponsors, broadcasters, officials and the game as a whole in the spirit of fair play.

THE KIDNAPPING BUSINESS
Rachel Briggs, The Foreign Policy Centre

The nature of kidnapping is changing: an important political tool is now a sophisticated business and the gap left by policy-makers has been filled by kidnap and ransom insurance. This project will assess these new trends and work towards a new integrated policy response. This project is supported by Hiscox, Control Risks Group, SCR, J&H Marsh and McLennan and ASM.

Subscribe to The Foreign Policy Centre

The Foreign Policy Centre offers a number of ways for people to get involved. Our subscription scheme keeps you up-to-date with our work, with at least six free publications each year and our quarterly newsletter, Global Thinking. Subscribers also receive major discounts on events and further publications.

TYPE OF SUBSCRIPTION	PRICE
● Individuals	£50
● Concessions (students, OAPs, JSA)	£25
● Organisations	£150
● Libraries (will receive ALL publications)	£200

Please make cheques payable to The Foreign Policy Centre, indicating clearly your postal and email address and the appropriate package and send to The Foreign Policy Centre, Panton House, 25 Haymarket, London SW1Y 4EN, or use the enclosed form.

The Foreign Policy Centre Diplomatic Partnership

The Foreign Policy Centre Diplomatic Partnership is aimed at the key embassy players. It is an ideal way for embassies to keep up to date with the work of The Foreign Policy Centre and will provide a useful environment for ideas sharing.

Members will receive the following benefits:

- Special invitations to attend The Foreign Policy Centre annual Diplomatic Forum, which will be led by a high-profile speaker, bringing together key embassy players to address one or more of the foreign policy issues of the day
- Three free copies of every Foreign Policy Centre publication
- Three free copies of *Global Thinking*, The Foreign Policy Centre's newsletter
- VIP invitations for up to three embassy representatives to all Foreign Policy Centre public events

Membership of The Foreign Policy Centre Diplomatic Partnership is £500 per year. Please contact Rachel Briggs for more details.

The Foreign Policy Centre Business Partnership

The Foreign Policy Centre also runs a Business Partnership scheme, which aims to bring the business community to the heart of foreign policy thinking.

For more details about this scheme, please contact Rachel Briggs, Fundraising Manager at rachel@fpc.org.uk

SUBSCRIPTIONS

Please Tick	Type of Subscription	Price
☐	Individual	£50
☐	Concessions (Students, OAPs, JSA) Please provide proof of status	£25
☐	Organisations	£150
☐	Libraries (will receive all Foreign Policy Centre publications)	£200
☐	Diplomatic Partnership (will receive all Foreign Policy Centre publications and be invited to attend annual Diplomatic Forum)	£500

PUBLICATIONS

No of Copies	Publication	Price
_____	The Foreign Policy Centre: **Mission Statement**	£1
_____	Held et al: **Globalization**	£4.95
_____	Ford/Katwala: **Making the Commonwealth Matter**	£4.95
_____	Leonard: **Network Europe**	£9.95
_____	Olins: **Trading Identities**	£9.95
_____	Ford/Katwala: **Reinventing the Commonwealth**	£9.95
_____	Leonard et al: **New Visions for Europe: Millennium Pledge**	£2.95
_____	Lloyd: **Re-engaging Russia**	£9.95
_____	Alibhai-Brown: **After Multiculturalism**	£9.95
_____	Leonard/Alakeson: **Going Public**	£9.95
_____	Worcester: **How to Win the Euro Referendum**	£9.95
_____	Edwards: **NGO Rights and Responsibilities**	£9.95
_____	Held: (prov) **Rethinking Sovereignty**	£9.95
_____	Katwala: **Democratising Global Sport**	£9.95
_____	Briggs: **The Kidnapping Business**	£9.95
_____	***Special Commonwealth Set*** *(2 pamphlets)* **Making the Commonwealth Matter** & **Reinventing the Commonwealth**	£12.95
_____ _____	***Special Europe Set*** *(3 pamphlets)* **How to win the Euro Referendum, Network Europe** & **New Visions for Europe**	£15.95

p&p = £1 per pamphlet (£1.50 per set)

PLEASE COMPLETE YOUR DETAILS OVERLEAF

FOR SUBSCRIPTIONS

please make cheque payable to
The Foreign Policy Centre and send to the Centre at

The Foreign Policy Centre
Elizabeth House
(The Mezzanine Floor)
39 York Road, London, SE1 7NQ
tel: 020 7401 5350
Email: info@fpc.org.uk

FOR INDIVIDUAL PAMPHLETS

please make cheque payable to Central Books and send to

Central Books
99 Wallis Road
London
E9 5LN
tel: 0181 986 5488,
fax: 0181 533 5821
email: mo@centralbooks.com

Please ensure that you include payment for p+p

PERSONAL DETAILS

Name: Ms/Mrs/Mr

Address

Postcode

Tel/Fax

E-mail

Organisation

The Foreign Policy Centre

www.fpc.org.uk